SUPER ONE-PAGE MATH COMICS

by Matt Friedman

S C H O L A S T I C
PROFESSIONAL **B**OOKS

New York · Toronto · London · Auckland · Sydney
· Mexico City · New Delhi · Hong Kong · Buenos Aires

Cover design by Gerard Fuchs
Interior design by Grafica, Inc.
Cover and interior illustrations by Miracle Studios

ISBN 0-439-15278-X

TABLE OF CONTENTS

Introduction

Whole Number Computation

Fractions and Decimals

TABLE OF CONTENTS

Geometry and Measurement

Mixed Skills

INTRODUCTION

WELCOME TO MATHTROPOLIS!

Enter an exciting, funny, comic-book city where crime-fighters rely as much on their math skills as their super powers! Different Math Team members review a variety of curricular skills in the comic strips. Then, your students help save the day by completing the problem set at the end of the comic and defeating the villain. Hey, how often do your students get to solve math problems and fight crime in the same day?

As students learn or review with each comic strip, you'll see them conquer the fears and insecurities they may have about math. Since many kids enjoy the comic strip and comic book forms, these pages will provide you with a great way to encourage students to improve their curricular skills.

During their adventures, your students will meet all six Math Team members. These Team members have diverse personalities and areas of math expertise. Plus, the activities and the characters' blend of action and humor have been carefully crafted to engage and empower girls and boys, math whizzes and math phobics.

By the end of the book, your students will have mastery over each hero's super math abilities, from whole number computation, fractions, and decimals to measurement and geometry . . . and beyond.

USING THIS BOOK

The activity pages are divided into four main sections: Whole Number Computation, Fractions and Decimals, Measurement and Geometry, and Mixed Skills. The table of contents gives you a breakdown of which Math Team Adventures fall into which general skill category.

The Skills Chart provides a more detailed list of which skills are highlighted in each activity. This chart also lists the supplementary skills needed to defeat the villain on any given page. Finally, this chart lists the National Council of Teachers of Mathematics (NCTM) standards to which each activity correlates. (A complete listing of the NCTM standards can be found on page 7.) Plus, if you want a quick reference for what skill is covered in a given activity, look no further than the top of the comic-strip page!

As mentioned above, the hero or heroes of each comic strip provide math instruction and work through a sample problem during their adventures. Then, the problem set gives students their chance to save the day!

The math skills covered become increasingly challenging as students work from the front of the book to its back. And within each problem set, the questions become progressively more difficult to build confidence, understanding, and, finally, mastery. Depending on your teaching goals for a given activity, you can even decide to allow students to use a calculator.

Looking for the perfect way to use the Math Team in your class? There are a number of approaches, including:

- Independent work (in class, as homework, or for a student's self-paced study)
- Small-group work (mini-Math Teams work together to find solutions)
- Whole-class work (your entire Math Team can work together to solve the problems)
- For fun (assign students to speak the parts of different characters from the comic strips)

WELCOME YOUR STUDENTS TO THE MATH TEAM!

A longtime comic-book reader and fan, and somewhat of a math-maniac, I've combined my two passions to create stories that students can both learn from and enjoy.

As your students begin their journey around the strange city of Mathtropolis, please tell them, "Welcome to the Math Team—we're counting on you!"

Matt Friedman

NCTM STANDARDS

Each Math Team Adventure corresponds with one or more of the teaching standards as delineated by the National Council of Teachers of Mathematics (NCTM). The following list excerpts NCTM's basic definitions of what instructional programs and materials for pre-kindergarten through grade 12 should enable students to do. Use this list, as well as the Skills Chart on page 9, to select pages and activities that will best fit the needs of your students.

1. NUMBER AND OPERATIONS STANDARD
- understand numbers, ways of representing numbers, relationships among numbers, and number systems;
- understand meanings of operations and how they relate to one another;
- compute fluently and make reasonable estimates.

2. ALGEBRA STANDARD
- understand patterns, relations, and functions;
- represent and analyze mathematical situations and structures using algebraic symbols;
- use mathematical models to represent and understand quantitative relationships;
- analyze change in various contexts.

3. GEOMETRY STANDARD
- analyze characteristics and properties of two- and three-dimensional geometric shapes and develop mathematical arguments about geometric relationships;
- specify locations and describe spatial relationships using coordinate geometry and other representational systems;
- apply transformations and use symmetry to analyze mathematical situations;
- use visualization, spatial reasoning, and geometric modeling to solve problems.

4. MEASUREMENT STANDARD
- understand measurable attributes of objects and the units, systems, and processes of measurement;
- apply appropriate techniques, tools, and formulas to determine measurements.

5. DATA ANALYSIS AND PROBABILITY STANDARD
- formulate questions that can be addressed with data and collect, organize, and display relevant data to answer them;
- select and use appropriate statistical methods to analyze data;
- develop and evaluate inferences and predictions that are based on data;
- understand and apply basic concepts of probability.

6. PROBLEM SOLVING STANDARD
- build new mathematical knowledge through problem solving;
- solve problems that arise in mathematics and in other contexts;
- apply and adapt a variety of appropriate strategies to solve problems;
- monitor and reflect on the process of mathematical problem solving.

7. REASONING AND PROOF STANDARD
- recognize reasoning and proof as fundamental aspects of mathematics;
- make and investigate mathematical conjectures;
- develop and evaluate mathematical arguments and proofs;
- select and use various types of reasoning and methods of proof.

8. COMMUNICATION STANDARD
- organize and consolidate their mathematical thinking through communication;
- communicate mathematical thinking and strategies of others;
- use the language of mathematics to express mathematical ideas precisely.

9. CONNECTIONS STANDARD
- recognize and use connections among mathematical ideas;
- understand how mathematical ideas interconnect and build on one another to produce a coherent whole;
- recognize and apply mathematics in contexts outside of mathematics.

10. REPRESENTATION STANDARD
- create and use representations to organize, record, and communicate mathematical ideas;
- select, apply, and translate among mathematical representations to solve problems;
- use representations to model and interpret physical, social, and mathematical phenomena.

SKILLS CHART

TITLE	PAGE	MAIN FOCUS	ADDITIONAL SKILLS	NCTM STANDARDS
Attributes of a Hero	10	Problem Solving, Attributes	Logic, Visual Discrimination	6,7,9,10
No Elbows on the Times Table	12	Whole Number Multiplication	Addition, Problem Solving	1,6,7,8
Divided We Fall	14	Whole Number Division	Multiplication, Measurement	1,6,8
The Average Joe	16	Averages (Arithmetic Mean)	Division, Problem Solving	1,2,6,7
Factor Fiction?	18	Factors of a Number	Multiplication, Division	1,6,8,9
Greatest Common Hacker	20	Greatest Common Factor	Division, Problem Solving	1,6,7,9
Least Common Criminals	22	Least Common Multiple	Multiplication, Patterns	1,6,7,8,9
Stolen Powers	24	Exponents	Multiplication, Factors	1,2,7
Fowl Fractions	26	Fraction Addition, Subtraction	Least Common Multiple	1,2,6,9
Lights! Camera! Fraction!	28	Fraction Multiplication	Simplest Form	1,2,6,7,9
The Incredible Shrinking Heroes	30	Reciprocals	Mixed Numbers, Improper Fractions	1,2,9
The Decimal Olympics	32	Decimal Addition	Place Value	1,2,4,6,7
Mass-sters of Decimals	34	Decimal Multiplication	Place Value, Problem Solving	1,2,4,6,8,9
Trouble's in Store	36	Money Computation	Decimal Addition, Multiplication	1,2,6,7
100% Danger!	38	Percent of a Number	Decimal Multiplication	1,2,6,9
Polly Gonn—Framed!	40	Names of Polygons	Visual Discrimination	1,3
Gone to Pieces	42	Tangrams	Visual Reasoning	3,6,7,10
Area in Underland	44	Area and Perimeter of Rectangles	Multiplication, Problem Solving	1–4,6–8
Sphere of Heights	46	Volume of a Sphere	Using a Formula, Pi	1,2,3,4,6,9
Take Me to Your Ruler	48	Measurement Equivalents	Basic Operations, Problem Solving	1,2,4,6,8–10
Blown Out of Proportion	50	Solving a Proportion	Scale, Ratio	1,2,4,6,8,9
Bugged by Pictographs	52	Reading, Making a Pictograph	Data Analysis, Basic Operations	1,2,5,6,9,10
Coordinated Clothing	54	Reading a Coordinate Grid	Following Directions	1,4,6
"x" Marks the Spot	56	Solving for Variables	Inverse Operations	1,2,6,7,9
Backward in Time	58	Working Backward	Problem Solving, Basic Operations	1,2,6,7,9

— Attributes of a Hero —

WELCOME TO THE MATHTROPOLIS CITY POLICE FORCE!

THIS FILE CONTAINS INFORMATION ABOUT THE HEROES YOU'LL BE WORKING SIDE BY SIDE WITH: THE MATH TEAM.

WE'VE GIVEN YOU A PHOTO OF EACH HERO, AND A LIST OF INFORMATION ABOUT THEIR NAMES AND ABILITIES. IN ORDER TO MAKE SURE THIS INFORMATION DOESN'T FALL INTO THE WRONG HANDS, WE'VE LEFT IT UP TO YOU TO MATCH THE NAMES AND ATTRIBUTES WITH THE PHOTOS.

BASED ON WHAT YOU LEARN FROM EACH PHOTO AND FROM THE CLUES, WRITE THE CORRECT HERO'S NAME AND EXACTLY 3 ATTRIBUTES OF THAT HERO IN THE CORRECT BLANKS.

HEROES' NAMES

Stat Cat

Jungle Jim, Calculating Ape

Ms. Mathlete

Polly Gonn, the Geome-Teen

Micro Man

Code Buster

HEROES' ATTRIBUTES

Has the athletic ability of a feline.

Secret identity is hockey star Monica Ruiz.

His inhuman speech is understood only by Micro Man.

On catching a criminal, often plays off his code name by saying the phrase, "You're busted!"

Can eat only flat foods, like crackers.

When removed from her belt, her mini vaulting pole and other sports items grow to full size.

Uses claws to scratch graphs and charts onto chalkboards, notepads, and even concrete walls.

Typically rides on one of Jungle Jim's shoulders.

The only English words he can say are numbers.

Is able to crack any code.

Wears a mask with ears to help protect her secret identity.

He may be small, but, like Ms. Mathlete's, his knowledge of foreign languages is large.

Comes from a world where all people are two-dimensional.

To prepare for meeting many people at the Olympics, she learned to speak many foreign languages.

Body appears to be made of various geometric shapes.

Can alter his height from 6 inches to 60 feet.

Beats the numbers on his chest to perform calculations.

Sometimes cracks cases with his parrot partner, Crackers.

1. Hero's Name: _____

   Hero's Attributes:

   a. _____

   b. _____

   c. _____

2. Hero's Name: _____

   Hero's Attributes:

   a. _____

   b. _____

   c. _____

MATH TEAM

3. Hero's Name: _____

   Hero's Attributes:

   a. _____
      _____
   b. _____
      _____
   c. _____

4. Hero's Name: _____

   Hero's Attributes:

   a. _____
      _____
   b. _____
      _____
   c. _____

5. Hero's Name: _____

   Hero's Attributes:

   a. _____
      _____
   b. _____
      _____
   c. _____

6. Hero's Name: _____

   Hero's Attributes:

   a. _____
      _____
   b. _____
      _____
   c. _____

Ms. Mathlete and Code Buster in . . .

No Elbows on the Times Table

MS. MATHLETE AND CODE BUSTER SUDDENLY FIND THEM-
SELVES TRANSPORTED ABOARD A STRANGE ALIEN SHIP!

I DO *NOT* LIKE THE WAY THESE CREATURES ARE LOOKING AT US, MS. MATHLETE!

ME EITHER, BUSTER. SUDDENLY, I KNOW HOW IT FEELS TO BE A *BIG MAC!*

MMM. WHY, SAW-TAY. IT'S ONLY YOUR FIRST DAY AS MY HEAD CHEF AND ALREADY YOU'RE FEEDING ME HUMANS. DELICIOUS!

NO, EMPEROR GLOO-TON—YOU MUST-N'T *EAT* THEM. THEY'RE HERE TO HELP ME *SERVE* YOU!

WORK FOR HIM? FORGET IT!

UH . . . MS. MATHLETE? MAYBE WE SHOULD PLAY ALONG WITH THEM Y'KNOW— FOR *NOW.*

PLEASE, MS. MATHLETE. YOU *MUST* HELP ME. AS HEAD CHEF, I MUST DETERMINE THE *EXACT* AMOUNT OF FOOD TO SERVE GLOO-TON AND HIS WARRIORS AT EACH MEAL. IF I SERVE EVEN A *LITTLE BIT* TOO MUCH OR TOO LITTLE, I—AND *YOU*—WILL BECOME THE EMPEROR'S NEXT MEAL!

EWWWWW! THEN WE'D BETTER GET STARTED.

THERE ARE 8 ALIENS WHO WILL EAT *ZELDORIAN EGGS.* EACH ALIEN GETS 3 EGGS.

SO, WE *MULTIPLY* 8 TIMES 3 TO FIND OUT HOW MANY EGGS WE'LL NEED IN ALL:
8 X 3 EGGS = 24 EGGS
LET'S START BY GIVING THIS FELLA *HIS* HELPING . . .

KEEP IT UP, GUYS—OR WE'RE TOAST!

MMM . . . TOAST.

No Elbows on the Times Table

SAVE THE DAY! Multiply the amounts in each question to make sure Ms. Mathlete, Code Buster, and Saw-Tay serve the correct amount of food. Now get cookin'!

1. A total of 6 aliens will drink Jupiter juice. Each alien should get 2 gallons of juice.

   A) What multiplication problem should you write to calculate how much juice they'll need in all? _____

   B) How many gallons of Jupiter juice will they need in all? _____

2. There are 5 aliens who will get moon pies. If each of them gets 7 pies, how many pies will be served in all? _____

3. Exactly 9 of the aliens will put asteroid salt on their Neptune noodles. Each needs 4 teaspoons of salt. How much salt will be served in all? _____

4. There are 3 aliens who will each want to eat 11 bowls of Mercury melon. How many bowls of melon will be served in all?

   _____

5. To keep themselves healthy, 10 warriors take Galac-C vitamins with dinner. If each warrior takes 7 vitamins, how many will they need in all? _____

6. If 12 warriors will have atomic turkey wings, and each alien gets 8 wings, how many wings should be served in all?

   _____

7. A total of 15 aliens will have Saturnian Ring-Ding donuts. If each alien gets 10 donuts, how many donuts must be served in all? _____

8. For dessert, Saw-Tay decides to serve B'henn and Jeh-Ree's Black Hole Crunch. Each warrior will get 18 pints. Gloo-Ton wants 23 times as much as each of his warriors. But a message on the label reads, "Warning: Eating more than 400 pints of Black Hole Crunch space cream may create a black hole that swallows you whole."

   A) Will Gloo-Ton eat enough Black Hole Crunch space cream to swallow him—and free our heroes? _____

   B) How many pints more or less would Gloo-ton need to eat to consume the fewest pints possible and still be swallowed by a black hole?

   _____

I CAN'T BELIEVE HE ATE THE HOLE THING!

The Math Team in . . .

Divided We Fall

GIVE IT UP, *DIVIDINI*. WE'RE RETURNING ALL THE MAGIC HATS AND RABBITS YOU'VE STOLEN, *AND* BRINGING YOU TO JAIL!

PUH-*LEASE!* YOU KNOW THAT, WITH MY SKILLS AS AN *ESCAPE ARTIST*, I CAN BREAK FREE OF ANY PRISON. BUT I'LL TELL YOU WHAT: I *PROMISE* TO TURN MYSELF IN, *AND* TO STAY IN JAIL, IF EACH OF YOU CAN ESCAPE FROM ONE OF MY DROPPING DIVISION TRAPS.

MAGIC HATS

NO *WAY* ARE WE GOING TO STEP INTO YOUR TRAPS!

POOF

WHO SAID YOU HAD A *CHOICE?*

DON'T *FRET*, HEROES. ALL YOU HAVE TO DO TO GET *FREE* IS SOLVE THE *DIVISION* PROBLEMS IN EACH OF YOUR TRAPS.

OF COURSE, YOU'LL BE A LOT BETTER OFF IF YOU CAN SOLVE THEM *BEFORE* YOU HIT THE GROUND.

IT'LL ONLY TAKE YOU 8 SECONDS TO FALL THE 1,024 FEET TO THE GROUND. WHAT WILL BE YOUR AVERAGE SPEED IN FEET PER SECOND? DIVIDE: 1,024 FEET ÷ 8 SECONDS =

BLAST! I CAN'T REACH MY SIZE CONTROLS. I'LL HAVE TO SOLVE HIS PROBLEM—AND FAST!

1,024 ÷ 8 = 128 FEET PER SECOND!

I'M FREE! BUT WHAT ABOUT THE REST OF MY TEAM?!

Divided We Fall

SAVE THE DAY! Help the heroes escape by solving the division problems written on their traps!

1. Polly Gonn: The mirror you're in has an area of 18 square feet. If it hits the ground, it (and you) will shatter into 2-square-foot pieces. How many pieces will you break into? Divide: 18 ÷ 2 = _____ 9 _____

2. Code Buster: The lock on your safe has numbers on it from 1 to 60. Say its 3-number combination to open it.

   A) The first number in the combination is 60 ÷ 5 = _____ 12 _____

   B) The second number: 60 ÷ 4 = _____ 18 _____

   C) The third number: 60 ÷ 10 = _____ 6 _____

3. Jungle Jim: You're wrapped in a total of 180 inches of chain.

   A) How many feet of chain is that? (Remember, 1 foot = 12 inches.)

   _____

   B) If you stretched out all of the metal in all of the links, they'd measure 420 inches long. If each link's length would be 14 inches, how many links must there be?

   _____

4. Stat Cat: Your tank will splatter 3,840 ounces onto the ground. How many cats will it take to drink up all of that water if each one has 8 ounces? _____

5. Ms. Mathlete: The barbells attached to your arms and legs have different weights on them. But the bars themselves each weigh 40 pounds.

   A) The one attached to your arms has a total weight of 670 pounds, including the bar. There are 14 discs of equal weight on the bar. How much does each disc weigh?

   _____

   B) The one attached to your legs weighs 310 pounds, including the bar. There are 18 discs of equal weight on the bar. How much does each disc weight?

   _____

6. For all of his crimes, Dividini is sentenced to a total of 1,890 days in jail. He stole 63 white rabbits and brown rabbits, and was sentenced an equal number of days for each one that he stole. How many days was each sentence?

   _____

WE DIVIDED—AND CONQUERED!

Ms. Mathlete in . . .

The Average Joe

YOU'RE GOOD, MS. MATHLETE . . . BUT THERE'S A REASON I'M THE LEAGUE'S MOST VALUABLE PLAY . . . *HUH?!*

SPROING!

WHAT *HAPPENED*, SLAM? YOU *NEVER* MISS AN EASY DUNK!

HE DOES *NOW*, THANKS TO ME!

SPUH-ROINGGG!

WHO IS *THAT?*

IT'S JOE MEAN— THE AVERAGE JOE!

JOE MEAN

THAT'S RIGHT. I'M USING MY POWERS TO CHANGE ALL OF BASKETBALL'S *SUPERSTARS* INTO *AVERAGE* SCORERS. *YOU* MUST CALCULATE THE *MEAN* NUMBER OF POINTS SCORED BY SLAM'S *TEAMMATES* IN THEIR MOST RECENT GAME. IF YOU FAIL TO DO SO BY GAME TIME TONIGHT, SLAM WILL *STAY* AN AVERAGE SCORER— FOREVER!

BUT OUR GAME STARTS IN JUST A *FEW* MINUTES!

WE'LL HAVE TO WORK FAST. TO CALCULATE THE MEAN OF A GROUP OF NUMBERS . . . FIRST ADD UP ALL THE NUMBERS IN THE SET. THEN DIVIDE BY THE NUMBER OF NUMBERS IN THE SET. *THAT QUOTIENT IS THE MEAN.*

LAST GAME, MY TEAMMATES SCORED 18, 23, 11, 4, 15, AND 29 POINTS. FIRST ADD: $18 + 23 + 11 + 4 + 15 + 29 = 100$ POINTS THEN DIVIDE: $100 \div 6 = 16.66666 . . .$ ROUNDED TO THE NEAREST TENTH, THAT'S 16.7 POINTS. *HEY*—IT WORKED! I'M BACK!

GREAT! NOW ALL I'VE GOT TO DO IS SAVE THE *OTHER* PLAYERS WHO'VE BEEN ATTACKED. THEN I'LL SETTLE THE SCORE WITH THE AVERAGE JOE!

The Average Joe

SAVE THE DAY! Don't let basketball's greatest scorers become average players. Calculate the average number of points scored by each player's teammates.

1. Next, Joe goes after Sue Wish. To save her, find the average of these scores: 15, 28, 17, and 25.

   A) What is the sum of the scores? _____

   B) How many scores are in the set?

   _____

   C) Divide your answer to **A** by your answer to **B**. (Don't forget to round to the nearest tenth!) Your answer to **C** is the average, or *mean*, of the scores.

   _____

2. Duncan DeBall has been attacked! Save him by finding the average of these teammates' scores: 27, 19, and 24.

   _____

3. Kent Miss can't make a shot unless you average these scores of his teammates: 7, 16, 27, 22, and 22.

   _____

4. Oops! Allie Oop missed another shot—and she'll keep missing unless you average these scores: 15, 9, 13, 31, 6, and 12.

   _____

5. Guy Kenshoot will keep throwing air balls until you find the average of these scores: 27, 14, 8, 18, 11, 20, and 14.

   _____

6. Reb Bounder can get the ball—but she can't shoot it well until you average these scores: 3, 10, 24, 6, 13, 18, 25, and 2.

   _____

7. Tip Inn should stay out of the game until you average these scores: 17, 5, 8, 14, 21, 5, 11, 9, and 8.

   _____

8. When Ms. Mathlete captures the Average Joe, she gives him the following puzzle: "The 7 players you attacked scored an average of exactly 35 points tonight. Here are 6 of the players' scores: 42, 29, 33, 41, 35, and 38. How many points did the seventh player score?" What should be Joe's answer? _____

WELL, *THAT* CERTAINLY WASN'T YOUR *AVERAGE* ADVENTURE!

Math TEAM

Stat Cat, Code Buster, and Polly Gonn in . . .

Factor Fiction?

Factor Fiction?

SAVE THE DAY! Answer the factor questions to prevent each person's stuff from being split into pieces.

1. Code Buster is trying to save Ray Dio's stereo. The question: Is 5 a factor of 40? _____

2. Stat Cat must protect Meg Ebite's computer. The question: Is 6 a factor of 34? _____

3. It's up to Polly to save Dee Cee's comic book collection. The question: Is 15 a factor of 345? _____

4. Buster will do his best to protect Flip Sover's stunt bike. The question: Is 21 a factor of 432? _____

5. Stat Cat's trying to save Lucky Braik's pool table. The question: Is 39 a factor of 624? _____

6. *Uh-oh!* Divider Dave is making the questions tougher as the heroes begin playing to save each other's stuff. First, Polly's playing for Buster's collection of Code Buster action figures. Circle the one number below that is *not* a factor of 42:

   1   2   3   6   7   12   14   21   42

7. Code Buster must protect Stat Cat's prized scratching post. Circle the three numbers below which are not factors of 63:

   1   3   6   7   9   13   21   33   63

8. Can Stat Cat save the Magi-cube that Polly Gonn calls home? To do so, she must list all of the factors of 48. What are they? _____

9. Sore loser that he is, Dave has one final challenge for you: He won't really give all of the stuff back in one piece unless you beat him in a race to list all of the factors of one more number: 60. Quick! List all the factors of 60! _____

10. As punishment for his crimes, Dave will be forced to spend one year (365 days) in jail watching reruns of bad game shows. He must watch each game show for an equal number of days, and must watch more than one show. What is the greatest number of days he could spend watching any one rerun?

    _____

CONSIDER DAVE'S SHOW *CANCELLED!*

Jungle Jim in . . .

Greatest Common Hacker

INSIDE MATH TEAM HEADQUARTERS, JUNGLE JIM SCANS THE CITY FOR ANY SIGNS OF DANGER, WHEN . . .

I, THE GREATEST COMMON HACKER, NOW CONTROL ALL OF THE MATH TEAM'S COMPUTERS! NOW, BEFORE YOU CAN GET ME OUT OF YOUR SYSTEM . . .

HRNNH? ROOGAH!

. . . I'LL BRING YOU INTO MINE! YOU'LL NEVER STOP THE E-VILLAINS I'VE SET AGAINST YOU. MEANWHILE, ONCE I'VE STOLEN ALL OF THE IMPORTANT CITY DATA FROM YOUR COMPUTERS, I'LL BE VIRTUALLY UNSTOPPABLE!

YOU'LL NEVER GET AWAY WITH . . . HEY! I CAN SPEAK ENGLISH. IT MUST BE SOME WEIRD SIDE EFFECT OF BEING PULLED INTO THE VIDEO GAME.

WHOA! I'M UNDER ATTACK BY THAT PUNKEMON HEAT-A-CHEW'S LIGHTNING BLASTS! AND THIS FIRE EXTINGUISHER ISN'T WORKING!

OF COURSE— THE GREATEST COMMON HACKER'S NAME SHOULD HAVE GIVEN HIM AWAY. THERE ARE NUMBERS BEING FORMED BY THE LIGHTNING BLASTS.

I'LL BET I NEED TO PICK THE FIRE EXTINGUISHER THAT HAS THOSE NUMBERS' GREATEST COMMON FACTOR, OR GCF, WRITTEN ON IT! THE GCF IS THE GREATEST FACTOR SHARED BY A GIVEN SET OF NUMBERS. FIRST, I'LL LIST ALL OF THE FACTORS OF EACH NUMBER. THEN I'LL FIND THE GREATEST NUMBER THAT'S A FACTOR OF BOTH!

FACTORS OF 12: 1, 2, 3, 4, 6, 12
FACTORS OF 16: 1, 2, 4, 8, 16
THE GCF OF 12 AND 16 IS 4.
I'M NOT BANANAS—IT WORKED!

EEP! I KNOW I HAVE TO DEFEAT THIS MONKEY GONG CHARACTER, BUT IT WOULD BE A LOT EASIER IF HE DIDN'T LOOK SO MUCH LIKE UNCLE GRUNK!

Greatest Common Hacker

SAVE THE DAY! Help Jungle Jim calculate the greatest common factor (GCF) of each number pair so he doesn't have a systems crash!

1. The Monkey Gong ape's barrels have the numbers 45 and 63 on them. A hammer that has the GCF of those two numbers on it can break all of his barrels.

   A) What are the factors of 45?

   _____

   B) What are the factors of 63?

   _____

   C) What is the GCF of 45 and 63?

   _____

2. Krush Handysnoot and Conic the Bed Hog both attack Jim. They're marked 20 and 15. What is their GCF that must appear on the boots Jim will use to kick these creatures away? _____

3. Two Digitmon characters numbered 16 and 24 try to blow Jim away with their blasts of wind. What GCF should be on the fan Jim uses to send the Digitmon flying? _____

4. Chomp-Man (numbered 35) and Ms. Chomp-Man (14) try to take a bite out of poor Jungle Jim. What is the GCF that should appear on the sour pellets that Jim feeds them? _____

5. Block Doom Raider's karate kicks with the GCF of 22 and 88! _____

6. Two Froggies marked 56 and 75 try to get the jump on Jim. What GCF must be on the net Jim uses to catch them? _____

7. Find the GCF of 78 and 117 to learn what number must be on the can of bug spray Jim uses to shoo Spider-Mutt! _____

8. A single meteor can stop Blasteroid ship numbers 84 and 57 if that meteor has what GCF written on it? _____

9. Three WWX wrestlers numbered 28, 42, and 98 try to body slam poor Jim. What referee shirt number should Jim put on to officially stop the fight? _____

10. The Greatest Common Hacker is purged from the Math Team's computer system when he fails to solve this final security puzzle. "To enter our data files, solve this: The GCF of 72 and this number is 8, and the second number is neither 8 nor 16. What is the lowest number we could be looking for?" The Hacker couldn't hack it. Can you? _____

GAME OVER!

The Math Team in . . .

Least Common Criminals

Least Common Criminals

SAVE THE DAY! Use the numerical clues in each question to calculate the LCM and help the heroes catch each Least Common Criminal! Start by listing the first five multiples of both numbers. If you don't find a common multiple, list a few more multiples of each.

1. Stat Cat spots a Least Common Criminal stealing tokens from a subway station for the 4 and 6 lines. Suddenly he splits into a dozen numbered nasties!

   A) List the first five multiples of 4:

   _____

   B) List the first five multiples of 6:

   _____

   C) The real Least Common Criminal is the one who's wearing the LCM of 4 and 6. What is the LCM? _____

2. Micro Man spots a Criminal stealing all the clocks that read 9:15 at the Second-Hand Clock Shop. Catch the clock criminal by finding the LCM of 9 and 15.

   _____

3. A Least Common Criminal tries to kidnap basketball player Kent Miss after he scored 27 points and had 9 rebounds in one game. To catch the real kidnapper, Ms. Mathlete must find the LCM of 27 and 9. _____

4. The street signs at the corner of 6TH Ave. and 22ND St. have been stolen by the criminal wearing the LCM of 6 and 22. What is their LCM? _____

5. One of the criminals stole thirteen 20-dollar bills from the Lowest Security Bank. But Jungle Jim can snag him by calculating the LCM of 13 and 20. _____

6. A criminal ran off with 14 gallons of ice cream from the 21 Flavors store! Help Code Buster stop him cold by calculating the LCM of 14 and 21. _____

7. The 3, 8, and 10 pins were stolen from Alley Cat's Bowling Bonanza. Help Polly pin down the real criminal by finding the LCM of 3, 8, and 10. _____

8. When the Least Common Criminals are sent to jail, each gets his or her own prisoner numbers. Two of the criminals get numbers that have an LCM of 78. One of the criminals' numbers is 26. The other's is a two-digit odd number. What is the second criminal's prisoner number?

   _____

LOOKS LIKE THOSE MULTIPLE MENACES WILL BE DOING *TIMES!*

The Math Team in . . .

Stolen Powers

CODE BUSTER, ARE YOU ALL RIGHT? HOW DID THIS GUY GET INTO OUR HEADQUARTERS?

HE STOLE MY CODE-BUSTING POWERS!

THAT'S *RIGHT.* I'M THE *POWER PLANT.* I USED MY EXPONENTIAL POWERS TO STEAL *BUSTER'S* POWERS. THEN I USED THEM TO CRACK THE *SECRET CODE* TO GET INTO YOUR HEADQUARTERS. I'LL KEEP *STEALING* HEROES' POWERS UNTIL I *RULE* THIS CITY!

$4^3 \; 2^5 \; 5^4 \; 7^2 \; 3^6$

INCREDIBLE! BY CHANTING EXPONENTIAL NUMBERS, HE'S STOLEN *ALL OF OUR* POWERS AND ABILITIES!

AND ONCE I'VE HAD YOUR POWERS FOR AN HOUR, THEY'RE MINE *FOREVER!* WITH THE MATH TEAM POWERLESS, THE TIME IS RIPE FOR ME TO . . .

STRIKE!

URNNNK!

LOOK OUT!

NOW, IF YOU'LL EXCUSE ME, I HAVE A CITY TO RULE!

HANG ON, JIM! GUYS—IF HE COULD *STEAL* OUR SUPER POWERS JUST BY SAYING *EXPONENTIAL* POWERS, MAYBE WE CAN GET THEM BACK BY *SAYING* THE NUMBERS IN *STANDARD* FORM!

AN EXPONENT TELLS HOW MANY TIMES A BASE NUMBER IS MULTIPLIED BY ITSELF. THE PLANT SAID 5^4 WHEN HE POINTED AT MICRO MAN.

THAT MEANS 5, THE *BASE,* IS MULTIPLIED BY ITSELF 4 TIMES: $5 \times 5 \times 5 \times 5 = 625$. SAY IT, MICRO MAN!

625!

IT'S *WORKING!* LET'S GET THE *REST* OF OUR POWERS BACK. THEN WE CAN *SHUT DOWN* THE POWER PLANT FOR GOOD!

Stolen Powers

SAVE THE DAY! Help the Math Team and other heroes get their powers back by writing the standard form of each exponential number.

1. To get Ms. Mathlete's powers back, find the standard form of 4^3.

   A) What is the base of 4^3?

   _____

   B) What is the exponent of 4^3?

   _____

   C) What equation must you write to calculate 4^3 in standard form?

   _____

   D) What is 4^3 in standard form?

   _____

2. Jungle Jim is just an ape who can't calculate until you figure out the standard form of 2^5. What is it? _____

3. Just purr-fect! Stat Cat has lost her cat-like powers and her statistics skills. They'll return if you determine the standard form of 7^2 = _____

4. Suddenly Polly Gonn is out of shape. Get her geometric powers back by finding the standard form of 3^6. _____

5. Code Buster's code-busting powers are a bust. Help him get back to full strength by finding the standard form of 8^4. _____

By the time the Math Team catches up with the Power Plant, he's stolen powers from three more heroes! Quick! Help them get back their powers before it's too late!

6. The Human Truck: 97^1 =

   _____

7. Iguanaman: 1^{50} =

   _____

8. Gum Girl: 285^0 =

   _____

9. The Team helps a total of 121 heroes get their powers back before they capture the Power Plant. How would you write 121 as an exponential number (and not as 121^1)?

   _____

10. Once the Power Plant goes to court, he is sentenced to 81 years in jail. Can you think of two ways to write 81 as an exponential number (and not as 81^1)?

   _____

NOW *THAT GUY* WAS *POWER MAD!*

Code Buster and Micro Man in . . .

Fowl Fractions

IN THE KITCHEN OF THE MATH TEAM'S HEADQUARTERS . . .

HEY, TURKEY! WHY HAVE YOU DRESSED UP *TURKEYS* TO LOOK LIKE OUR *TEAMMATES*? WHERE ARE THE *REAL* HEROES?

LOOK OUT FOR THAT *BASTER*, BUSTER!

CALL ME THE *FOWL PLAYER*. AS FOR WHAT I'VE DONE TO YOUR *FRIENDS* . . .

. . . DOES *THAT* ANSWER YOUR QUESTION?

GOBBLE!

AAAA!

NONE OF YOUR FRIENDS WAS ABLE TO FOLLOW MY *FRACTION* RECIPES FOR MAKING THE *PERFECT* TURKEY DINNER. IF *YOU* FAIL, YOU WILL STAY A *BIRDBRAIN*, TOO. DO A *GOOD* JOB AND I'LL TURN THEM BACK TO *NORMAL*.

I'LL TURN BUSTER BACK TO NORMAL—*FOR NOW*. BUT ONE MISTAKE, AND YOU'RE BOTH OUT OF *CLUCK*—ER, LUCK. NOW, PUT $\frac{2}{3}$ CUPS MORE *FLOUR* THAN *BACON BITS* INTO MY *GRAVY* MIXTURE. THERE'S $\frac{1}{4}$ CUP OF BACON BITS IN THE GRAVY.

WE'LL DO THE *BASTE* WE CAN!

WHOA! THAT WAS FOR THE BIRDS!

TO *ADD* TWO FRACTIONS, FIND THE *LEAST COMMON MULTIPLE* OF THE TWO DENOMINATORS—THE *LOWEST COMMON DENOMINATOR* (LCD). THEN *RENAME* BOTH FRACTIONS SO EACH HAS THE LCD AS ITS DENOMINATOR. ONCE YOU'VE RENAMED BOTH FRACTIONS, *ADD* THE NUMERATORS AND PUT THE SUM OVER THEIR COMMON DENOMINATOR.

SO, WE HAVE TO *ADD* $\frac{1}{4} + \frac{2}{3}$ TO FIND OUT HOW MUCH *FLOUR* WE'LL NEED. THE LCD OF 4 AND 3 IS 12.

$$\frac{1}{4} \times \frac{3}{3} = \frac{3}{12}$$
$$\frac{2}{3} \times \frac{4}{4} = \frac{8}{12}$$
$$\frac{3}{12} + \frac{8}{12} = \frac{11}{12}$$

WE'LL NEED $\frac{11}{12}$ OF A CUP OF FLOUR.

GOOD! NOW GET COOKING—OR BECOME VICTIMS OF *FOWL PLAY*!

Fowl Fractions

SAVE THE DAY! Calculate how much of each food that the Fowl Player wants in his fraction feast.

1. The Fowl Player always puts $\frac{2}{5}$ of a pound more chocolate chips than marshmallows in his salad. He used $\frac{1}{2}$ of a pound of marshmallows. Add the two fractions to find out how many pounds of chocolate chips to use.

   A) What is the lowest common denominator (LCD) of the two fractions? (Remember: Find the least common multiple of 5 and 2.) _____

   B) Rewrite both fractions so each has the LCD as its denominator. _____

   C) Add the two fractions. _____

2. He likes to eat $\frac{7}{12}$ of a bowl of sardine soup, followed by $\frac{1}{6}$ of a bowl more of Swiss-cheese soup. Add $\frac{7}{12}$ and $\frac{1}{6}$ to find out what fraction of a bowl of Swiss-cheese soup to serve. _____

3. The Fowl Player likes $\frac{7}{8}$ of a teaspoon of brown sugar in his sweet potatoes, and $\frac{3}{4}$ of a teaspoon less of honey in them. What is $\frac{7}{8} - \frac{3}{4}$? _____

4. It takes $\frac{1}{3}$ of an hour to preheat the oven, then $\frac{4}{7}$ of an hour more than that to bake the sweet potatoes. What is $\frac{1}{3} + \frac{4}{7}$?

   _____

5. The Fowl Player tells Buster to fill a glass $\frac{4}{9}$ of the way with cider, then another $\frac{1}{6}$ of the way with potato juice. What is $\frac{4}{9} + \frac{1}{6}$? _____

6. Once the turkey is done, the Fowl Player eats $\frac{5}{11}$ of one leg, then $\frac{3}{10}$ of the other. How much less of the second leg did he eat than he did of the first? _____

7. For dessert, the Fowl Player wants $\frac{7}{15}$ of a pumpkin pie and $\frac{3}{10}$ of a pecan pie. What total fraction of a pie will he eat?

   _____

8. The Fowl Player is so happy with the heroes' cooking, he turns the rest of the Math Team back into humans. After dropping the Player off to live on a farm, the Team sits down to finish the meal. Stat Cat eats $\frac{5}{9}$ of a plate of food. Micro Man eats $\frac{5}{12}$ less of a plate than that. Jim eats $\frac{13}{18}$ more of a plate than Micro did. What fraction of a plate of food did Jim eat? _____

I GUESS ALL'S WELL THAT *EATS* WELL!

Ms. Mathlete and Stat Cat in . . .

Lights! Camera! Fraction!

RRROWR! WHAT HAPPENED, MS. MATHLETE? ONE MINUTE, WE WERE WATCHING CURSE OF THE SCAREWOLF *ON TV . . . NOW WE'RE* INSIDE *THE MOVIE!*

I, FRITZ FRACTION, *HEAD OF FRACTION FEATURES, HAVE CAST YOU IN MY* ULTIMATE HORROR FILM. *YOU'LL BATTLE THE GREATEST HORROR MOVIE* VILLAINS *OF ALL TIME!*

STAT CAT, YOU'VE STILL GOT THE REMOTE CONTROL. *ZAP US* OUT *OF HERE!*

DON'T DO SOMETHING YOU'LL REGRET. *SOMEWHERE ON THE SCREEN IS A* FRACTION MULTIPLICATION *PROBLEM.*

ITS ANSWER IS THE ONLY *CHANNEL NUMBER YOU CAN SAFELY PRESS. HIT THE* INCORRECT *NUMBER AND YOU'LL BE TRAPPED IN THAT MOVIE . . . FOREVER!*

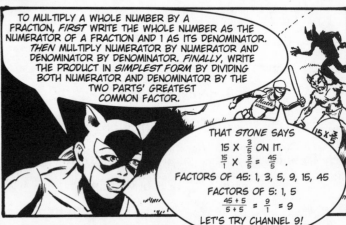

TO MULTIPLY A WHOLE NUMBER BY A FRACTION, FIRST *WRITE THE WHOLE NUMBER AS THE NUMERATOR OF A FRACTION AND 1 AS ITS DENOMINATOR.* THEN *MULTIPLY NUMERATOR BY NUMERATOR AND DENOMINATOR BY DENOMINATOR.* FINALLY, *WRITE THE PRODUCT IN* SIMPLEST FORM *BY DIVIDING BOTH NUMERATOR AND DENOMINATOR BY THE TWO PARTS' GREATEST COMMON FACTOR.*

THAT STONE *SAYS* $15 \times \frac{3}{5}$ *ON IT.*

$$\frac{15}{1} \times \frac{3}{5} = \frac{45}{5}.$$

FACTORS OF 45: 1, 3, 5, 9, 15, 45

FACTORS OF 5: 1, 5

$$\frac{45 \div 5}{5 \div 5} = \frac{9}{1} = 9$$

LET'S TRY CHANNEL 9!

HEY, WE'RE ON THE SET OF MESS-A-ME STREET! *WE'LL BE SAFE HERE!*

HEY, STINKALOTAMUS! LET'S SAY "HELLO" TO OUR NEW FRIENDS!

MESS-A-ME ST.

BRAVO, HEROES. BUT I THINK OUR AUDIENCE *WOULD MUCH RATHER SEE YOU ON CHANNEL 17.*

CHANNEL 17? BUT THAT'S *WHERE THEY'RE SHOWING . . .*

. . . THE FRACTION-STEIN MONSTER!

Lights! Camera! Fraction!

SAVE THE DAY! Don't just sit there eating popcorn! Multiply fractions to help Ms. Mathlete and Stat Cat pick safe channel numbers!

1. As the *Fraction-stein* monster attacks, Ms. Mathlete spots this multiplication problem on an operating table: $\frac{4}{7} \times 28$. Follow these directions to figure out which channel number they should hit:

A) Write 28 as a fraction with 1 as its denominator. _____

B) Multiply numerator times numerator, and denominator times denominator.

_____

C) Divide numerator and denominator by their greatest common factor (GCF).

_____

D) Your final answer is the product in its simplest form. If its denominator is one, rewrite the numerator as a whole number.

_____

2. On Channel 31 Stat Cat and Ms. Mathlete are chased by the slimy, cloth-wrapped Scummy! Pick the channel number they should go to next by multiplying $\frac{1}{4} \times 84$.

_____

3. Next, Ms. Mathlete and Stat Cat appear inside the movie *Drabula, Lord of the Badly Dressed Vampires*! There, they see the problem $\frac{5}{9} \times 27$. To what channel number can they safely escape? _____

4. Our heroes visit *The Sixth Cents*, where ghosts walk around jingling loose coins! They can escape by pressing the channel number that equals $\frac{7}{8} \times 32$. _____

5. While being attacked by big-brained zombies in *Night of the Living Head*, Ms. Mathlete and Stat Cat get away by solving this problem: $\frac{3}{10} \times 80$. _____

6. Giant dinosaur dogs attack in a scene from *Jurassic Bark*! Change that channel by solving $\frac{4}{12} \times 6$. _____

7. Stat Cat convinces a witch from the movie *Which Witch Is Which?* to cast a spell that traps Fritz in the TV . . . and sets Stat Cat and Ms. Mathlete free! Fritz must multiply 30 by a fraction to get a product of 14. The heroes then leave Fritz inside an episode of *Blarney, the Lucky Green Dinosaur* until the police arrive. What fraction must Fritz multiply by 30 to get 14? _____

AND *CUT.* THAT'S A WRAP!

The Incredible Shrinking Heroes

Code Buster, Polly Gonn, and Jungle Jim in . . .

The Incredible Shrinking Heroes

SAVE THE DAY! The fractions below show the factor by which the Living Doll has shrunken different people. Find the reciprocal of each one so our heroes can bring the person back to full size—that is, if they can get past the cat!

1. Polly Gonn: Find the reciprocal of $\frac{3}{7}$

   A) First, flip the numerator and the denominator: _____

   B) If the answer to **A** is an improper fraction, write it as a mixed number:

   _____

   Your answer to **B** should be $\frac{3}{7}$'s reciprocal!

2. Code Buster: Find the reciprocal of $\frac{2}{11}$.

   _____

3. Jungle Jim: Find the reciprocal of $\frac{4}{17}$.

   _____

4. Lois Hite: Find the reciprocal of $\frac{1}{6}$.

   _____

5. Luke Ameeshrenk: Find the reciprocal of $\frac{5}{18}$. _____

6. Lil Shorter: Find the reciprocal of $\frac{12}{25}$.

   _____

7. Jim grabs one of the robot cat's whiskers, swings onto its back, and forces the cat to bring the heroes to the Living Doll. Polly jumps onto the shrinking ray, points it at the cat, and sets it to $31\frac{2}{3}$. The cat grows so large that the Doll must reduce it to normal size before it smushes him. What's the reciprocal of $31\frac{2}{3}$? _____

8. Polly uses the ray to return Mrs. Gleeful to normal size. Then Polly quickly sets it to $7\frac{3}{11}$ and points it at Mrs. Gleeful. Now about 40 feet tall, Mrs. Gleeful captures the Living Doll. Now she wants to get back to normal size. What's the reciprocal of $7\frac{3}{11}$? _____

To Find a Mixed Number's Reciprocal:

Convert the mixed number into an improper fraction.

Then flip the numerator and the denominator.

Example: $4\frac{2}{9} = \frac{38}{9}$

$\frac{38}{9} \longrightarrow \frac{9}{38}$

WE ARE *NOT* TO BE TOYED WITH!

Micro Man in . . .

The Decimal Olympics

MICRO MAN, I CAN'T THANK YOU ENOUGH! ONLY YOU, WITH YOUR AMAZING POWERS, CAN HELP US!

NO THANKS ARE NECESSARY. I'M GLAD I CAN . . .

. . . JUDGE THE EVENTS AT YOUR DECIMAL OLYMPICS! WHOA!

YOU'LL BE IN CHARGE OF CALCULATING WHO GETS THE GOLD MEDALS BASED ON EACH COMPETITOR'S SCORES IN THE DIFFERENT EVENTS. WE'RE JUST IN TIME FOR THE ROLL VAULT FINALS!

YOU MUST ADD UP THE TOTAL DECIMAL HEIGHTS THAT EACH COMPETITOR JUMPS IN ALL THREE OF THEIR TRIES.

AMAZING— HE MADE IT, .172 METERS!

SOON . . .

LEE PURR JUMPED .172, .095, AND .15 METERS. HI JUMPARR VAULTED .125, .13, AND .164 METERS. TO CALCULATE THE TOTAL DISTANCE EACH JUMPED, FIRST LINE UP THE DECIMAL POINTS. TO MAKE FOR EASIER ADDING, I'LL PLACE ZEROES TO THE RIGHT OF THE DECIMALS THAT DON'T HAVE AS MANY PLACES.

LEE	HI
.172	.125
.095	.130
+ .150	+ .164
.417	.419

SINCE .419 IS GREATER THAN .417, HI JUMPARR WINS!

IF YOU CAN KEEP THIS UP FOR THE REST OF THE COMPETITIONS, YOU'LL DESERVE A MEDAL, MICRO MAN!

The Decimal Olympics

SAVE THE DAY! Help Micro Man add and subtract decimals to determine the winner of each Decimal Olympic event!

1. The women's .75-meter runners finished in these times:

   A) Millie Meedur: 13.351 sec., 12.84 sec.

   Total time: _____

   B) Lilly Puht: 13.2 sec., 12.98 sec.

   Total time: _____

   C) Which runner had the *lower* time?

   _____

   D) By how many seconds did she win?

   _____

2. Next up is the javelin competition (using toothpicks).

   A) Farrah Throwah: .29 m, .354 m

   Total distance: _____

   B) Luke Attitgoe: .339 m, .302 m

   Total distance: _____

   C) Whose total throws went further and by how far? _____

3. In the weight-lifting competition, hard candies are put onto a stale, licorice bar for contestants to try to carry. Calculate the total weight lifted by each finalist.

   A) Sue Purstrongh: .085 lbs., .11 lbs.

   Total weight: _____

   B) Carrie Allot: .106 lbs., .09 lbs.

   Total weight: _____

   C) Who lifted more and by how many pounds (lbs.)? _____

4. The uneven parallel bars are made of toothbrush poles and bars of dental floss. Jim Nesticks scored a 9.925, but got .23 points taken off for making mistakes during his routine. Flip Ohverr scored a 9.875, but had .178 points taken off for his mistakes. Who had the higher score after the deductions, and by how many points did he win? _____

5. The final event of the day is the discus-throwing (actually *N&N-candy*-throwing) competition. Only .00015 meters separated the first- and second-place finishers. Which scores could have been from the top pair? Circle the correct answer.

   A) .25684 to .40684

   B) .25684 to .25669

   C) .25684 to .25579

   D) .25684 to .25834

THEY WERE THE *NUMBER .1* ATHLETES IN THE WORLD!

The Math Team in . . .

The Mass-sters of Decimals

THE MATH TEAM HAS TRACKED THE MASS-STERS OF MENACE TO A SECRET **MATHA*** BASE...

OH, NO! IT'S THE MATH TEAM. THEY'VE FOUND US!

QUICKLY! WE'LL LOSE THEM BY SPLITTING UP. EACH OF US WILL TELEPORT TO A DIFFERENT PLANET.

THEY'RE GETTING AWAY!

*****MATHA:** **M**ULTINATIONAL **A**EROSPACE **T**RANSPORTATION **H**EADQUARTERS **A**REA

THAT'S OK. EVERYONE ACTIVATE YOUR SPACE GEAR. THEN INPUT YOUR WEIGHT INTO A TELEPORTATIONAL DEVICE AND IT'LL TAKE YOU TO THE SAME PLANET AS ONE OF THE MASS-STERS!

THAT PLAN MAKES SENSE. SO WHY DO I HAVE SUCH A BAD FEELING IN MY STOMACH?

WOW! PLUTO! IT FIGURES *I'D* END UP ON THE SMALLEST PLAN...AAA!!

ZZZAP!

NOW THAT *YOU'RE* HERE, I—AND THE REST OF THE MASS-STERS—WILL TELEPORT BACK TO EARTH. THERE, WE'LL DESTROY THE TELE-PORT MACHINES, TRAPPING YOUR ENTIRE TEAM IN SPACE FOREVER! TOO BAD YOU PROBABLY DON'T KNOW WHAT YOUR WEIGHT IS ON PLUTO, OR YOU MIGHT'VE MADE IT BACK!

NOOOOOO! I CAN'T LET HIM DESTROY THOSE MACHINES! I MUST INPUT MY CORRECT WEIGHT ON THIS PLANET.

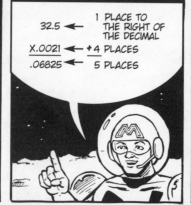

TO FIND AN OBJECT'S WEIGHT ON PLUTO, MULTIPLY ITS EARTH WEIGHT BY .0021. WHEN MULTI-PLYING WITH DECIMALS, COUNT THE TOTAL NUMBER OF PLACES TO THE RIGHT OF THE DECIMAL IN BOTH FACTORS. THAT'S HOW MANY PLACES SHOULD BE TO THE RIGHT OF THE DECIMAL IN THE PRODUCT. I WEIGH 32.5 POUNDS ON EARTH WHEN I'M THIS HEIGHT.

$$
\begin{array}{rl}
32.5 & \leftarrow \quad 1 \text{ PLACE TO THE RIGHT OF THE DECIMAL} \\
\underline{\times .0021} & \leftarrow \quad +4 \text{ PLACES} \\
.06825 & \leftarrow \quad 5 \text{ PLACES}
\end{array}
$$

BACK ON EARTH...

ONE OF THEM MADE IT BACK. STOP HIM, QUICKLY!

MADE IT! NOW, IF ONLY I CAN HOLD OFF THE MASS-STERS UNTIL THE OTHERS GET BACK—IF THEY GET BACK!

The Mass-sters of Decimals

SAVE THE DAY! The chart tells you what to multiply an object's Earth weight by to get its weight on other planets. Calculate the weight that each hero must input into her or his teleporter to get back to Earth.

MULTIPLY OBJECT'S EARTH WEIGHT BY . . .	TO GET OBJECT'S WEIGHT ON . . .
.38	MERCURY
.91	VENUS
.38	MARS
2.36	JUPITER
.92	SATURN
.89	URANUS
1.12	NEPTUNE
.0021	PLUTO

1. Stat Cat is trapped on Neptune!

A) By what factor should she multiply her Earth weight to find her weight on Neptune? _____

B) If she weighs 150 pounds on Earth, what does she weigh on Neptune? _____

2. Jungle Jim is stuck on Venus! He weighs 280.3 pounds on Earth. What weight must he type into the teleporter to get back to Earth? _____

3. Polly Gonn is stranded on Saturn! Being two-dimensional, she only weighs 65.2 pounds on Earth. What is her weight on Saturn? _____

4. Code Buster is in jeopardy on Jupiter. He weighs 185.69 pounds on Earth. What weight must he type into the teleporter?

_____

5. Bring Ms. Mathlete back from Mars. She weighs 162.54 pounds on Earth. What does she weigh on Mars? _____

6. The Math Team returns before the Mass-sters can destroy the teleporters. Now, the villains teleport to Uranus. The Math Team, except for Micro Man, teleports after them. The Mass-sters weigh 148, 194, 206, 159, 179, and 185 pounds on Earth. They all jump onto one teleporter, and destroy the rest. What was their combined weight on Uranus? _____

7. Micro Man places the last Earth teleporter into a jail cell, trapping the villains upon their return! Since the five Math Team members have only one teleporter to use now, what is their combined weight on Uranus? _____

On separate paper: What would *your* weight be on each of the other planets?

WHEN I WAS STUCK ON JUPITER, I COULDN'T *WEIGHT* TO GET BACK!

Stat Cat, and Jungle Jim, the Calculating Ape, in . . .

Trouble's in Store

Trouble's in Store

SAVE THE DAY! Calculate each hero's total bill. Line up the decimals of each amount before adding or subtracting.

1. The Human Thumb needs to get her hands on:

   5-gallons of nail polish **$25.00**

   1 tube of Blisterex hand balm **$16.00**

   Total cost: _____

2. To avoid injury, Kid Klutz gets:

   Non-slip shoes **$9.00**

   Water-proof utility belt **$11.25**

   Elbow pads **$6.50**

   Total cost: _____

3. Ally Gator, girl crocodile, chooses these snappy items:

   Bionic tail **$28.75**

   Super-strength dental floss **$3.50**

   Cold-blood heating kit **$9.75**

   Total cost: _____

4. Fire-Breathing Flounder buys these hot items:

   Super-powered chili peppers **$17.95**

   Flame-breath minimizer **$33.29**

   Fire extinguisher **$24.48**

   Total cost: _____

In problems 5 and 6, heroes purchase more than one of the same item. First multiply each item's price by the number of that item being purchased. Add up the total amounts spent on each item to get the total cost.

5. Bug-Eyed Girl improves her peepers with:

   Heat vision glasses **$7.39** $\times$ 4 = _____

   Eyesine eye drops **$2.95** $\times$ 6 = _____

   Total cost: _____

6. Gar Bahj, the human trash heap, picked:

   Ultra-Odor Tamers **$8.35** $\times$ 12 = _____

   Fresh-cut flowers **$4.89** $\times$ 7 = _____

   Fly repellent **$5.61** $\times$ 6 = _____

   Total cost: _____

7. And what happened to the villain who caused this mess—the Overloader? He was put in jail, and charged $89.71 to pay for the several copies of *Maps to the Super Heroes' Homes* and *The Book of Super Heroes' Weaknesses* that he stole. If maps cost $7.25 each, and books cost $16.99 each, how many of each had the Overloader stolen? _____

   _____

> THE STORE EVEN GAVE ME A DISCOUNT FOR HELPING OUT!

Stat Cat in . . .

100% Danger!

100% Danger!

SAVE THE DAY! Calculate each percentage that Statis-Trisha asks for to help Stat Cat deactivate the Data-bots!

1. Statis-Trisha sends her kangaroo-bots against Stat Cat next. Only 57% of the 74 kangaroo-bots can kick-box. Stat Cat must calculate 57% of 74.

A) Rewrite 57% as a decimal. _____

B) Multiply that decimal by 74. _____

C) Round to the nearest whole number. That's the number of kangaroo-bots that can kick-box—and the number that will deactivate them! _____

2. Lucky for Stat Cat, only 20% of the 80 vampire bat-bots have fangs! What is 20% of 80? _____ *60%* _____

3. Even if only 14% of the 35 rhino-bots have horns, they're still hard to dodge! What's 14% of 35? _____

4. A panel slides out from underneath Stat Cat, dropping her into a pool of water filled with piranha-bots! Luckily, only 8% of the 145 piranha-bots have teeth. What's 8% of 145? _____

5. Just as Stat Cat tried to climb out of the water, she was attacked by octo-bots. Exactly 59% of the 134 octo-bots can squirt blinding ink into the water. What's 59% of 134? _____

6. Those panda-bots may look cute, but 71% of the 55 of them are karate experts! What's 71% of 55? _____

7. Out of 354 spidery arachno-bots, 28% can spin webs, but that's still enough to make a sticky situation for Stat Cat! What's 28% of 354? _____

8. After defeating the last of these robots, Statis-Trisha still says she's the city's best super-statistician. *Then* Stat Cat points out that Statis-Trisha incorrectly calculated what percentage of her total number of robots were bee-bots. In shame, Statis-Trisha promises to give herself up to the police. Add up the total number of robots from the questions plus the number of bee-bots. What percentage of the total number of robots were actually bee-bots?

_____

IT ISN'T EASY TO *BEE* THE BEST!

Stat Cat, Code Buster, and Polly Gonn in . . .

Polly Gonn—Framed!

THERE MUST BE SOME *MISTAKE.* THERE'S NO *WAY* POLLY GONN DESTROYED THOSE GREAT WORKS OF ART!

I'M SORRY, *STAT CAT.* THE SHAPES OF ALL THE PAINTINGS WERE CHANGED INTO STRANGE *POLYGONS.* POLLY'S THE *ONLY* PERSON ON EARTH WHO CAN DO THAT.

DON'T *WORRY,* POLLY. WE'LL PROVE YOUR INNOCENCE *SOMEHOW.*

THANKS, BUSTER. IN THE MEANTIME, USE MY *POLY-TRON RAY* TO CHANGE THE ART BACK TO NORMAL. JUST INPUT THE NAME OF EACH PICTURE'S *CURRENT SHAPE* AND SET THE *POLY-TRON* TO "REVERSE."

WILL DO. TAKE CARE!

SOON, AT THE ART EXHIBITION . . .

THESE SHAPES ARE SO *WEIRD.* HOW ARE WE SUPPOSED TO KNOW WHAT THEY'RE CALLED?

EASY. YOU CAN IDENTIFY A *POLYGON* BY THE NUMBER OF *ANGLES* IT HAS. SEE?

POLYGON NAME	NUMBER OF ANGLES
TRIANGLE	3
QUADRILATERAL	4
PENTAGON	5
HEXAGON	6
HEPTAGON	7
OCTAGON	8
NONAGON	9
DECAGON	10

THAT *KNOWLEDGE* WON'T HELP YOU NOW!

WHO . . . ?

I'M *MISS SHAPEN,* AND I COME FROM THE SAME *DIMENSION* AS YOUR FRIEND, *POLLY.* ONLY I'VE *POLY-GONE* BAD!

FIRST, I FRAMED *POLLY.* AND NOW I'VE FRAMED CODE BUSTER, *TOO.* HAHAHAHAHAHA!

MAYBE. BUT NOW THAT I KNOW THE SECRET TO *NAMING* POLYGONS, I CAN *END* YOUR GEOMETRIC *MAYHEM.*

Polly Gonn—Framed!

SAVE THE DAY! While Stat Cat struggles to get the Poly-tron back from Miss Shapen, help her by writing the new polygon shape for each painting's frame.

• •

1. *The Mona Lisa* by Leonardo Da Vinci is now in a frame with 5 sides:

_____

2. *American Gothic* by Grant Wood has a 7-sided frame:

_____

3. *Dove of Peace* by Pablo Picasso is squeezed into a 3-sided frame:

_____

4. *The Persistence of Memory* by Salvador Dali now has 10 sides:

_____

5. *Sky City Pottery* by Kass Morin Freeman has 9 sides: _____

6. *Dog Barking* by Keith Haring has 6 sides:

_____

7. *The Scream* by Edvard Munch is surrounded by 8 sides:

_____

8. *Campbell's Soup* by Andy Warhol now with 10 sides:

_____

9. And finally a 5-sided *Code Buster* by Miss Shapen:

_____

10. Stat Cat wrestles the Poly-tron away from Miss Shapen! Before Stat Cat can use the ray to change the art back to normal, she traps Miss Shapen in a 12-angled picture frame. To find out the name of a 12-angled polygon, fill in the blanks below as follows: Under each blank is a number and a letter indicator. The number tells you which problem number's answer you'll take the letter from. The letter indicator tells you which letter (from left to right) from the answer to write on that blank.

What do you call a 12-angled polygon?

___	___	___	___	___	___	___	___	___
#4	#2	#8	#1	#7	#1	#6	#5	#3
1st letter	7th letter	1st letter	2nd letter	2nd letter	5th letter	5th letter	6th letter	5th letter

I'M GLAD WE STRAIGHTENED OUT THAT MESS!

Polly Gonn and Code Buster in . . .

Gone to Pieces

Gone to Pieces

SAVE THE DAY! A Tangram is a seven-piece puzzle made up of five triangles, a parallelogram, and a square. The puzzle is believed to have been created hundreds of years ago in China. Photocopy this page, or trace the square Tangram design and its dotted lines. Glue the entire square onto a piece of cardboard. Cut the Tangram along the dotted lines. Then use those pieces to form the shapes of the people, animals, and objects Tan Graham has turned into Tangrams, so they can return to normal. You will need to use all seven pieces to create each design.

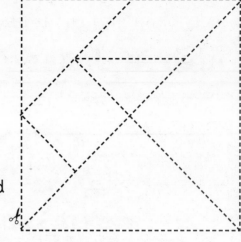

1. When Tan first got his powers, he accidentally zapped his pet cat.

2. Tan wanted to show off his new powers to his little brother, who was playing soccer at the time. You can guess what happened . . .

3. Late one night, Tan spotted a couple of suspicious-looking men throwing something off the side of a sailboat. Before Tan realized they were just throwing the *anchor*, he had transformed the entire boat.

4. During a power outage, Tan used a candle to see his way around the house. When the power came back on, he tried to blow out the candle and . . .

5. Tan accidentally locked himself out of his house one day. He meant to turn only the front door into a Tangram . . .

6. Hey! Tan snagged an actual criminal who was running from the store he had just robbed! Check him out.

7. This poor rabbit made the mistake of digging holes in Tan's backyard!

8. Finally, Tan returns everything back to normal! But he gets clumsy while celebrating in front of a mirror . . .

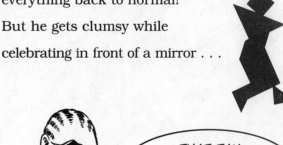

THAT TAN GRAHAM WAS A REAL CRACK-UP!

Polly Gonn and Ms. Mathlete in . . .

Area in Underland

I'M LATE. I'M *LATE!* I'M LATE TO *CALCULATE!* PERIMETER = 18 FEET. AREA = 20 SQUARE FEET.

HEY, HOW DID THAT GUY GET INTO OUR HEADQUARTERS? AND *WHAT* IS HE DOING TO OUR FLOOR?!

WE'LL HAVE TO *FOLLOW* HIM TO FIND OUT. RACE YOU TO THE . . .

5'   4'

. . . BOTTOMMMM!

WHOA!

UGH!!

WHUNFF!

IT *APPEARS* WE HAVE GUESTS. I AM THE *MAD ADDER.* YOU'RE *WELCOME* TO STAY FOR TEA *IF* YOU TELL ME THE *PERIMETER* AND *AREA* OF MY TABLETOP!

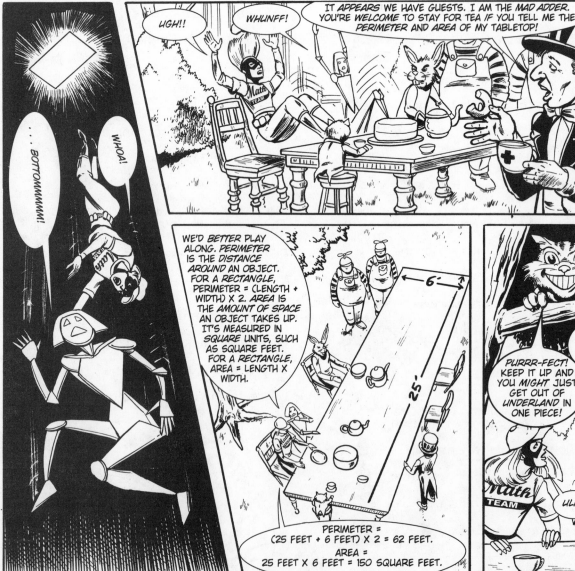

WE'D *BETTER* PLAY ALONG. *PERIMETER* IS THE *DISTANCE AROUND* AN OBJECT. FOR A *RECTANGLE*, PERIMETER = (LENGTH + WIDTH) X 2. *AREA* IS THE *AMOUNT OF SPACE* AN OBJECT TAKES UP. IT'S MEASURED IN *SQUARE UNITS*, SUCH AS SQUARE FEET. FOR A *RECTANGLE*, AREA = LENGTH X WIDTH.

6'

25'

PERIMETER = (25 FEET + 6 FEET) X 2 = 62 FEET.
AREA = 25 FEET X 6 FEET = 150 SQUARE FEET.

GOOD WORK, MATHLETE.

PURRR-FECT! KEEP IT UP AND YOU *MIGHT* JUST GET OUT OF *UNDERLAND* IN ONE PIECE!

ULP!

Area in Underland

SAVE THE DAY! Calculate the perimeter and area of the rectangle in each problem so Polly Gonn and Ms. Mathlete can escape from Underland.

1. Before the heroes are allowed to leave the Mad Adder's table, they must calculate the perimeter and area of Tweedledeep and Tweedledunce's rectangular bellies. Tweedledeep's has these measurements: length (l) = 3 feet, width (w) = 7 feet.

   A) What equation would you set up to calculate this rectangle's perimeter (P)?

   _____

   B) What is P?_____

   C) What equation would you set up to calculate this rectangle's area (A)?

   _____

   D) What is A?_____

   Tweedledunce's rectangle has these measurements:

   l = 2 feet, w = 5 feet.
   E) P = _____
   F) A = _____

2. After leaving the table, Polly and Ms. Mathlete come upon a giant forest. There, a huge caterpillar rests on a mushroom that has a rectangular top. The caterpillar says it will let them by if they can calculate the perimeter and area of the top of its mushroom. l = 6 feet, w = 8 feet.
   A) P = _____
   B) A = _____

3. Next, they try to follow a mouse into its tiny house to ask for directions. But they can't fit through its tiny door! A sign tells them that they'll be able to shrink down to the right size if they can calculate the perimeter and area of the rectangular door. Here l = 17 inches and w = 3 inches.
   A) P = _____
   B) A = _____

4. The mouse promises to give them directions home if they solve a rectangle puzzle that will make the Pester Cat stop chasing him. They must calculate the perimeter and area of a rectangle where l = 14 feet and w = 16 feet.
   A) P = _____
   B) A = _____

5. The mouse forgot to mention that Polly and Ms. Mathlete had to walk through the Queen of Horrors' kingdom on their way home. The Queen, who wears a huge playing card on her back (no one knows why), tells them that the card's area is 1,215 square inches. If its l = 45 inches, what is w?_____

6. Then, the queen makes the two heroes stand on a huge checker board and act like playing pieces until they can answer a couple of questions. If the entire square board's area is 576 square feet, what is its length?

   _____

7. To get out of Underland through a mirror, the heroes must answer one final question for the mirror. w = 45 inches, P = 144 inches. What is l?

   _____

IT'S A WONDER WE GOT OUT OF THERE!

Jungle Jim and Micro Man in . . .

Sphere of Heights

RUNK GLOOP SNEEE RUMPLE OOK!

WHAT DO YOU MEAN THOSE AREN'T HOT AIR BALLOONS, JIM? LET ME SEE!

YOU'RE *RIGHT.* THEY'RE HUGE *SPHERICAL* PEOPLE! THEY'VE GOT WEIRD *GADGETS* ATTACHED TO THEM WITH A *RADIUS* WRITTEN ON EACH ONE'S *SCREEN.* THE GADGETS MUST'VE BLOWN THE PEOPLE UP LIKE *BALLOONS!*

THAT'S RIGHT. I—*INFLATE-A-BILL*—HAVE GIVEN ALL THESE PEOPLE A *DREAM-COME-TRUE.* THEY CAN *FLY!* TOO BAD THEY CAN'T *LAND*—UNLESS YOU CAN FIND THE *VOLUME* OF EACH FLOATING FOOL. TAH-TAH!

JIM!!!

VOLUME (V) IS THE AMOUNT OF SPACE A 3-D OBJECT TAKES UP. IT'S MEASURED IN *CUBIC UNITS,* SUCH AS CUBIC FEET. TO FIND THE VOLUME OF A *SPHERE,* USE THE FORMULA $V = \frac{4}{3}\pi R^3$ (AND π = ABOUT 3.14).

THE GADGET SAYS YOUR RADIUS IS 6 FEET. $V = \frac{4}{3} \times \pi \times 6 \times 6 \times 6 = 904.32$ CUBIC FEET. LET ME PUNCH THAT NUMBER INTO THE *DEVICE . . .*

AROONKA LUG CHUGGA URNK!

NO NEED TO *THANK* ME OLD FRIEND. NOW WE BETTER CATCH THE *REST* OF THESE FLOATING FOLKS BEFORE THEY GO INTO ORBIT!

Sphere of Heights

SAVE THE DAY! Flying a police chopper, Jungle Jim and Micro Man take to the skies to save each puffed-up person. Read the person's name and radius. Find the volume so the people can be reduced to their normal sizes. Use 3.14 as an estimate for π. Round your answers to the nearest hundredth. And don't forget to include the units!

1. Before Inflate-a-Bill struck, Kent Land was having a ball at a party. Now he *is* a ball—a big flying one! His radius (r) = 3 feet.

   A) What equation would you set up to find the volume (V) of Kent's sphere body?

   _____

   B) V = _____

2. Ella Vayshun has always wanted to fly. But she thought it would be in an airplane, not like this! If r = 5 feet, V = _____

3. People always told Al T. Tude that he had his head in the clouds. It's finally true! If his r = 10 feet, V = _____

4. Balloon shop owner Izzie Fline finally knows what it feels like to be one of the toys she sells. If her r = 7 feet, V = _____

5. Look, up in the sky! It's a bird! It's a plane! Nope, it's just N. DeSky slowly heading into space! If r = 13 feet, V = _____

6. Lee R. Jett is a great all-around athlete. Now he's just all around! If r = 18 feet, V = _____

7. Ann T. Grevitee loves the view from 1,000 feet up. Of course, she wishes she knew how to get down! If r = 23 feet, V = _____

8. Micro Man and Jim have cornered Inflate-a-Bill inside a local store. The plan is to plant one of his own devices on him, and inflate him so big that he'll be trapped in the building, but not be hurt. To do that, his *diameter* will have to be 38 feet. What would be Inflate-a-Bill's volume?

   _____

LOOKS LIKE INFLATE-A-BILL WAS FULL OF *HOT AIR!*

Micro Man in . . .

Take Me to Your Ruler

AT A UNITED NATIONS ASSEMBLY . . .

UNLESS WE CONTINUE TO CLEAN THE WORLD'S WATER SUPPLIES . . .

ZAP

I'M ALL FOR HELPING THE ENVIRONMENT, BUT ALL THIS TALK SURE DOESN'T MAKE FOR THE MOST EXCITING GUARD DUT... HUH?!

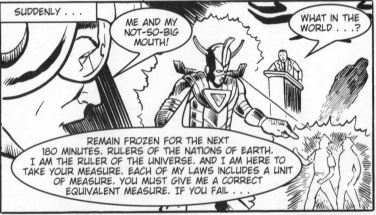

SUDDENLY . . .

ME AND MY NOT-SO-BIG MOUTH!

WHAT IN THE WORLD . . .?

REMAIN FROZEN FOR THE NEXT 180 MINUTES. RULERS OF THE NATIONS OF EARTH. I AM THE RULER OF THE UNIVERSE. AND I AM HERE TO TAKE YOUR MEASURE. EACH OF MY LAWS INCLUDES A UNIT OF MEASURE. YOU MUST GIVE ME A CORRECT EQUIVALENT MEASURE. IF YOU FAIL . . .

I WILL BE YOUR RULER, AND THE LAWS I READ WILL BE YOUR LAWS FOREVER! SO, LET US BEGIN WITH AN EASY WARM-UP QUESTION: RULER OF NORWAY, FOR HOW MANY HOURS HAVE I FROZEN THE GUARDS?

NUTS! MANY OF THESE RULERS DON'T USE THIS SYSTEM OF MEASUREMENT IN THEIR COUNTRIES. THEY MAY NEED MY HELP.

THE RULER SAID FOR THE GUARDS TO FREEZE FOR 180 MINUTES. AND 1 HOUR = 60 MINUTES. TO FIND HOURS, DIVIDE: 180 ÷ 60 = 3.

THE ANSWER IS . . .

THE ANSWER IS 3 HOURS!

GOOD. VERY GOOD!

THE NORWEGIAN GOT THE ANSWER ON HIS OWN. BUT I'D BETTER CHECK EVERYONE'S WORK, JUST IN CASE. WE CAN'T AFFORD A SINGLE MISTAKE!

Take Me to Your Ruler

SAVE THE DAY! Calculate the equivalent measure in each problem to help make sure the Ruler of the Universe leaves our world alone!

1. If the Ruler of the Universe takes over our world, humans will be forced to work 1,380 minutes per day.

   A) What equation would you set up to find out how many hours equal 1,380 minutes? _____ (Remember, 1 hour = 60 minutes.)

   B) How many hours equal 1,380 minutes? _____

2. The Ruler of the Universe's favorite drink is Earth's diesel fuel. Humans would be required to serve him 1,740 quarts per day. How many gallons is that? (1 gallon = 4 quarts.) _____

3. Each human would be required to lift 3,024 ounces at a time as workers in the rock mines. How many pounds is that? (1 pound = 16 ounces.) _____

4. The Ruler of the Universe isn't entirely heartless—each worker gets a day off once every 1,008 hours. How many days apart is each human's day off? (1 day = 24 hours.) _____

5. The Ruler will even let a human retire from work once they're 33,215 days old. How many years old is that? (1 year = 365 days; ignore leap years.) _____

6. That's enough talk about rest! Each human will be required to walk at least 89,760 feet each way to and from his or her work location. How many miles is that? (1 mile = 5,280 feet.) _____

7. Thinking of rebelling? Don't! The Ruler's computers know what you're planning before you even think it! After all, the computer in his big toe alone has 98,566,144 bytes of memory! How many megabytes is that? (1 megabyte = 1,048,576 bytes.) _____

8. Satisfied with our measurement skills, the Ruler has agreed to leave our planet alone. But he's too dangerous to other planets to be let go. So, Micro Man quickly grows to a huge size, and a weight of 11 tons. Micro then puts his giant foot down on the Ruler, holding him there until he can be disarmed. How many pounds did Micro Man weigh when he stepped on the Ruler? (1 ton = 2,000 pounds.) _____

LOOKS LIKE WE *MEASURED UP* TO ANOTHER CHALLENGE!

Micro Man and Ms. Mathlete in . . .

Blown Out of Proportion

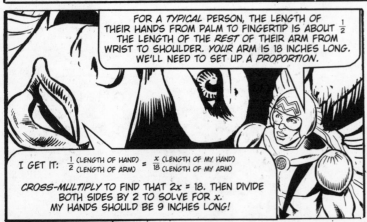

Blown Out of Proportion

SAVE THE DAY! Help Micro get the other people's body parts back to normal size by using proportions!

1. Poor Sarah Bellum's head is so big, she's standing on it! The height of a person's head is usually about $\frac{1}{8}$ of her total height. Sarah's normal height is 56 inches. How many inches tall should Sarah's head be?

   A) What proportion should you set up to find the length of Sarah's head? _____ _____

   B) What should be the length of Sarah's head? _____

2. Micro goes to the aid of Guy Zundheit, whose nose has been made tremendous by Al. The length of a person's nose is usually about $\frac{3}{14}$ the length of his head. If Guy's head is 9.1 inches long, how long should his nose be? _____ _____

3. Iris Pupil's eyes are now gigantic! Each eye is usually about $\frac{1}{5}$ the width of someone's entire face. If Iris's face is 5.5 inches wide, how wide should her eyes be? _____ _____

4. It looks like Han Stand is all thumbs! A person's thumb is usually about $\frac{5}{7}$ as long as his index finger is. If Han's index finger is 2.8 inches long, how long should his thumb be? _____

5. And Pierce Eng is all ears! The height of a person's ears is usually about $\frac{2}{7}$ the height of his entire head. If Pierce's head is 9.1 inches tall, how tall should his ears be?

   _____

6. Fifi Murr's forearms are tremendous! The length of a person's forearms is usually about $\frac{1}{1}$ the length of her foot. If Fifi's foot is 7.2 inches long, about how long should her forearms be? _____

7. Meanwhile, Ham Streng's legs are like stilts! The length of a person's legs is usually about $\frac{8}{15}$ of his total height. If Ham's total height is usually 66 inches, about how long should his legs be? _____

8. Ms. Mathlete can't dodge Disproportion Al's disproportion rays for much longer. So, Micro Man sneaks in and grows a dollar bill to $\frac{240}{1}$ of its original length, blanketing Al and preventing him from using his powers. If a normal dollar bill is 6.125 inches long, how many *feet* long is the bill with which Micro Man covered Al? _____

I GUESS AL JUST COULDN'T HANDLE *BIG* MONEY.

The Math Team in . . .

Bugged by Pictographs

HELP US, MATH TEAM! OUR DEPARTMENT HAD JUST LEARNED THAT THE *EMPIRE ANTS* ARE PLANNING TO *INVADE* THE CITY. BUT THOSE BLASTED *BUGS* FOUND OUT WE WERE ON TO THEM AND ARE TAKING US *CAPTIVE!*

IT'S UP TO *YOU* TO STOP THE INVASION!

I'M DOWNLOADING A PICTOGRAPH THAT SHOWS THE *LOCATIONS* EACH INVASION FORCE WILL ATTACK, AND THE NUMBER OF *MILLIONS* OF ANTS IN EACH SQUAD. *PROTECT* THE CITY. YOU'RE OUR ONLY *HOPE!*

WE *WON'T* LET YOU DOWN, CHIEF!

How Many Ants Will Attack Each Area of the City

Key ⚡ = 1,000,000 Ants   ⚡ = 500,000 Ants

Center City: ⚡⚡⚡⚡⚡⚡⚡⚡⚡⚡⚡⚡⚡
The Hub: ⚡⚡⚡⚡⚡⚡⚡⚡⚡⚡⚡⚡⚡⚡⚡⚡⚡⚡⚡⚡⚡⚡⚡⚡
Middle Park: ⚡⚡⚡⚡⚡⚡⚡⚡⚡⚡⚡⚡⚡⚡⚡⚡⚡⚡⚡⚡
Big Central Station: ⚡⚡⚡⚡⚡⚡⚡⚡⚡⚡⚡⚡⚡⚡⚡⚡⚡⚡⚡⚡⚡⚡⚡⚡⚡⚡⚡⚡⚡
The Marina: ⚡⚡⚡⚡⚡⚡⚡⚡⚡⚡⚡⚡⚡⚡⚡⚡

IT DOESN'T LOOK LIKE IT'LL BE SO HARD, BUSTER.

LET'S HOPE WE CAN *KEEP* THAT PROMISE, MS. MATHLETE.

THAT *GRAPH* DOESN'T SHOW ANYWHERE NEAR *MILLIONS* OF ANTS.

YES IT *DOES*, MICRO. IN A PICTOGRAPH, EACH PICTURE STANDS FOR A LARGER NUMBER OF OBJECTS.

WE'RE GETTING THE *PICTURE*, STAT CAT. ITS *KEY* IS THE KEY TO FIGURING OUT HOW MANY ANTS ARE IN EACH AREA.

Bugged by Pictographs

SAVE THE DAY! Answer the questions to determine how many ants will attack different areas of the city.

1. Which area will be attacked by the fewest ants? _____

2. According to the key . . .

A) each 🐜 stands for how many ants? _____

B) each 🐜 stands for how many ants? _____

3. How many ants will attack . . .

A) the Marina? _____

B) Middle Park? _____

4. How many more ants will attack . . .

A) Big Central Station than the Marina? _____

B) the Hub than Center City? _____ _____

5. Big Central Station will be invaded by twice as many ants as which other area? _____

6. How many ants will attack the city in all? _____

7. If just one super hero can stop 500,000 ants, how many heroes would it take to stop all of those ants? _____

8. The Team decides that there's only one way to stop the ant invasion: Lure the ants into giant picnic baskets and trap them inside. To get the ants into the baskets, they'll need the following foods to fill them: 700 bananas, 550 PB&J sandwiches, 400 hot dogs, 250 bags of chips. Use the information in the key to complete the pictograph so it shows how many of each item the Math Team will need. We did one for you.

How Many of Each Food Item Needed

Key 🧺 = 100 items 🧺 = 50 items

Bananas: 🧺 🧺 🧺 🧺 🧺 🧺 🧺 _____

PB&J Sandwiches: _____

Hot Dogs: _____

Bags of Chips: _____

I ALWAYS COUNT ON GRAPHS TO HELP ME OUT!

Code Buster, Jungle Jim, and Stat Cat in . . .

Coordinated Clothing

CLOTHING CRIMINAL MANNY KENN'S TRAIL LEADS OUR HEROES TO A STRANGE WAREHOUSE . . .

WE *KNOW* THAT ONE OF THESE MANNEQUINS IS THE REAL *YOU*, MANNY. YOU MAY AS WELL DROP THE *CLOTHES* YOU'VE STOLEN AND GIVE UP!

I DON'T THINK SO! YOU'LL HAVE TO FIGURE OUT WHICH MANNEQUIN IS ME. BUT IF YOU EVEN *TOUCH* THE WRONG WELL-DRESSED DUMMY . . .

JIM, BE CAREFUL!

. . .YOU'LL BECOME A *FASHION VICTIM!*

GASP!

NOOOO!

WANT TO CATCH THE *REAL ME*? READ EACH COORDINATE PAIR THAT I'VE LISTED ON THE *BACK* OF YOUR APE-FRIEND'S *CAPE*. THEN FIND THAT *ORDERED PAIR* ON THE COORDINATE GRID. ONCE YOU'VE DONE *THAT* FOR ALL OF THE CLUES, YOU'LL GET A DESCRIPTION OF THE WELL-COORDINATED *OUTFIT* THAT ONLY *I* AM WEARING.

COORDINATES, HUH? TO LOCATE POINTS ON THE *GRID*, WE'LL HAVE TO USE THE *ORDERED PAIRS* MANNY GAVE US. THE *FIRST* POINT TO FIND IS (5, -2). THE *FIRST* NUMBER TELLS US HOW MANY POINTS TO MOVE ALONG THE HORIZONTAL *X*-AXIS. THE *SECOND* NUMBER TELLS US HOW MANY POINTS TO MOVE ALONG THE VERTICAL *Y*-AXIS.

THE LETTER "*B*" IS AT THAT POINT! MANNY, I HOPE YOU LIKE HOW YOU LOOK IN *PRISON STRIPES!*

Coordinated Clothing

SAVE THE DAY! Match each ordered pair below to its point on the coordinate grid. Write the letter that appears at that point in the blank above the ordered pair to find out what the real Manny is wearing!

· ·

____ ____ ____ ____   ____ ____ ____ ____ ____
(5, -2) (-3, -2) (-5, 1) (-2, -3)   (1, -5) (4, 2) (-4, 3) (3, -4) (6, 4)

____ ____ ____ ____ ____ ____ ____   ____ ____ ____ ____ ____ ____
(3, -4) (-2, 4) (-4, 3) (0, 3) (5, -2) (4, -6) (-3, 5)   (1, -5) (4, 2) (4, -6) (3, -4) (6, 4) (1, -5)

____ ____ ____   ____ ____ ____ ____ ____ ____ ____ ____ ____ ____
(-2, 4) (0, 3) (-4, -5)   (1, -5) (-5, 1) (0, 3) (-6, 6) (-3, -2) (-2, 4) (1, -5) (1, -5) (-2, -3) (1, -5)

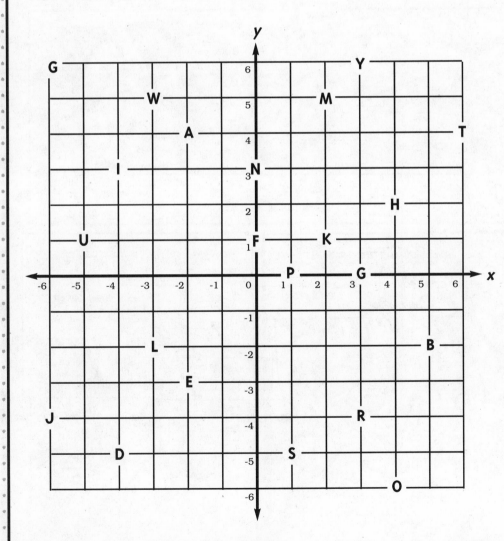

Don't Stop Now: To turn Jungle Jim back to normal, help Code Buster and Stat Cat create a set of coordinate clues that spell out the words "MAKE JIM AN APE AGAIN."

THAT ADVENTURE REALLY *WORE* ME OUT!

Code Buster and Jungle Jim in . . .

"x" Marks the Spot

ABOVE A SOUTH AMERICAN JUNGLE, TREASURE HUNTER ANNE THROWPOLOGEE HOLDS TWO UNHAPPY CAPTIVES!

ONLY YOU CAN DECIPHER THE VARIABLE CLUES TO GET PAST HIS TRAPS IN THE CAVES BELOW. AND THE ONLY WAY I'LL LET YOU BACK OUT IS IF YOU RETURN WITH HIS TREASURE. BYE-BYE FOR NOW!

THERE'S NO WAY WE'LL HELP YOU FIND THE PIRATE X-BEARD'S MISSING TREASURE!

URRNK!

YAAAAAAAAA!

WHUMP!

GRUNNK!

NICE SAVE, JIM!

WE'LL HAVE TO DO WHAT ANNE WANTS . . . FOR NOW!

HEY, HERE'S THE FIRST CLUE. IT SAYS THE ANCIENT STATUE OF PRINCE HOT'TAH FIRES A BURNING BEAM OF LIGHT FROM ITS EYES EVERY s SECONDS, WHERE 3s + 9 = 33. HOW MANY SECONDS APART IS THAT? LET'S SEE. TO SOLVE FOR s, FIRST "UNDO" ADDITION AND SUBTRACTION. THEN "UNDO" MULTIPLICATION AND DIVISION.

CAREFUL, JIM! FIRST, "UNDO" THE ADDITION BY SUBTRACTING 9 FROM BOTH SIDES.

$$3s + 9 = 33$$
$$\underline{-9-9}$$
$$3s= 24$$

THEN WE "UNDO" THE MULTIPLICATION BY DIVIDING BOTH SIDES BY 3.

$$\frac{3s}{3} = \frac{24}{3} \quad \text{SO, } s = 8$$

CHECK THE ANSWER BY PLUGGING IT INTO THE ORIGINAL EQUATION:
$3(8) + 9 = 33$
$24 + 9 = 33$. IT CHECKS OUT! MORE BEAMS WERE JUST FIRED. WE'VE GOT 8 SECONDS BEFORE THE NEXT ONE. C'MON!

ZAP!

ERRRN. ERRRN!

"x" Marks the Spot

SAVE THE DAY! Solve the variable equation clues to get Code Buster and Jungle Jim past each trap and to the treasure!

1. Watch your step! There are trap doors every f feet on the floor, where $f = 91 \div 7$. One wrong move and it's into a snake pit for Buster and Jim! How many feet apart are the trap doors? _____

2. Huge stone doors fall, sealing the heroes into part of the cavern. The ceiling begins to fall towards them. A set of weights lie on the floor next to a scale. On the wall, it says to place p pounds on the scale to make the doors open before they're crushed, where $2p - 23 = 57$.

A) First, undo addition and subtraction. What should be done to both sides? _____
_____

B) Then, undo multiplication and division. What should be done to both sides? _____
_____

C) How many pounds (p) should be put on the scale? _____

3. To work a primitive elevator, Buster and Jim must use a 1-gallon jug to fill a larger bucket with g gallons of water, and then pull a lever. Adding the right amount of water brings the elevator to the correct level. If they're wrong, they'll fall into a bottomless pit. How many gallons of water should they put in the bucket if $g \div 5 = 6$? _____

4. A 10-mile-span of lava separates them from the next part of the cave. On a wall, it says that the bridge over the pit will disappear in h hours, where $13 = 7h - 1$. How long do Buster and Jim have before it disappears? _____

5. The treasure is in sight! A sign says that deadly tarantulas come out to protect it every m minutes, where $30 = m \div 11 + 29$. If the tarantulas just attacked, how long do Buster and Jim have to grab it before the spiders strike again? _____

6. Anne throws down a rope ladder so that Jim and Buster can bring the treasure chest to the top of the pit. Anne pulls at its lock, ignoring the message on it: "Carry the chest at least d miles from the cave before opening. $41 = 4d \div 9 + 13$." The chest opens, pulls Anne and her crew in, and locks them inside. How many miles must Jim and Buster move the chest to open it again so they can put Anne and her crew in jail? _____

I'LL TREASURE THIS ADVENTURE FOREVER.

Polly Gonn and Code Buster in . . .

Backward in Time

IN THE LAB OF MAD GENIUS, BECK N. TIME . . .

CODE BUSTER, YOU AND YOUR MATH TEAM HAVE PLAGUED ME FOR TOO LONG. IT'S TIME FOR THAT TO CHANGE. SEE YOU LATER—I MEAN, EARLIER! HAHAHA!

WE'RE TOO LATE, POLLY!

YOU'RE RIGHT, BUSTER. WITH HIS TIME-TRAVEL EQUIPMENT, BECK COULD CHANGE HISTORY!

WE CAN STILL CATCH BECK. HE LEFT BEHIND A "WORKING BACKWARD" PROBLEM AS A CLUE!

HEY, YOU'RE RIGHT! IT SAYS HERE, "MY SECOND TIME-JUMP WILL TAKE ME BACK 10 TIMES AS MANY YEARS IN THE PAST AS MY FIRST JUMP. MY FIRST TIME-JUMP WILL TAKE ME BACK 2 YEARS."

THE END OF THE PROBLEM SAYS BECK FIRST JUMPED 2 YEARS INTO THE PAST. HIS SECOND JUMP TOOK HIM 10 TIMES AS MANY YEARS INTO THE PAST AS HIS FIRST JUMP DID. SO, HIS SECOND JUMP WAS 2 X 10, OR 20 YEARS. TO FIND OUT HOW MANY YEARS HE'S TRAVELED IN ALL, ADD 20 + 2 TO GET 22 YEARS.

BUT WHAT COULD HE WANT 22 YEARS IN THE PAST? I GUESS WE'LL FIND OUT ONCE WE GET THERE.

WHY WOULD BECK HAVE TAKEN HER KID?

MY BABY! THAT MONSTER STOLE MY SON!

MA'AM, CAN YOU TELL US YOUR SON'S NAME?

IT'S BUSTER. BUSTER BARON.

MOM?

Backward in Time

SAVE THE DAY! Beck N. Time is trying to stop Code Buster's crime-fighting career before it even begins. Solve Beck's working-backward problems—or Code Buster is history!

1. Beck left this clue in the hospital: "To find baby Buster, you'll have to travel 3 times as many miles south as you'll travel west. You'll need to go west 19 miles." How many miles south should they go? _____

2. On arriving at the secret location, Buster and Polly find a small building that's only entrance is an unbreakable safe door with a combination lock. This clue is on the door: "The last number in the combination is $\frac{1}{5}$ of the previous number. That number is 37 more than the first number. The first number is 23." What's the . . .

   A) second number in the code? _____

   B) third number in the code? _____

3. Buster enters the safe door. Inside are a scale and three babies. They all look exactly like baby Buster. A note reads, "Take the wrong baby from this room, and you'll be sorry! The real Buster weighs 9 ounces less than the fake one that has a memory-zapping ray in it. The memory-zapping baby weighs 1 pound, 10 ounces more than the fake one that has hypnotic eyes. The hypnotic-eyed baby weighs 8 pounds, 5 ounces." How much does the real baby Buster weigh? _____

4. From a hidden control room, Beck cackles, "You didn't really think I'd let you get away, did you?" As his finger is poised to press a button that will set off all the fake babies' traps, Polly bursts into the room. It takes her $\frac{1}{2}$ as long to deactivate the fake babies as it did for her to take down Beck. But it only took her $\frac{1}{6}$ as long to stop Beck as it did to get the real baby back to his mother. And it took about 2.5 times as long to get the baby back to his mom as it did for Buster and Polly to set the time machine to bring them back to the exact time they wanted. It took them 24 minutes to set the time machine. How long did it take Polly to deactivate the fake babies? _____

THAT'S ALL THE TIME WE HAVE FOR NOW, FOLKS. SEE YA!

Answers

PAGE 11

1. Code Buster

a) On catching a criminal, often plays off his code name by saying the phrase, "You're busted!"

b) Is able to crack any code.

c) Sometimes cracks cases with his parrot partner, Crackers.

2. Stat Cat

a) Has the athletic ability of a feline.

b) Uses claws to scratch graphs and charts onto chalkboards, notepads, and even concrete walls.

c) Wears a mask with ears to help protect her secret identity.

3. Polly Gonn, the Geome-Teen

a) Can eat only flat foods, like crackers.

b) Comes from a world where all people are two-dimensional.

c) Body appears to be made of different geometric shapes.

4. Micro Man

a) Typically rides on one of Jungle Jim's shoulders.

b) He may be small, but, like Ms. Mathlete's, his knowledge of foreign languages is large.

c) Can alter his height from 6 inches to 60 feet.

5. Ms. Mathlete

a) Secret identity is hockey star Monica Ruiz.

b) When removed from her belt, her mini vaulting pole and other sports items grow to full size.

c) To prepare for meeting many people at the Olympics, she learned to speak many foreign languages.

6. Jungle Jim, Calculating Ape

a) His inhuman speech is understood only by Micro Man.

b) The only English words he can say are numbers.

c) Beats the numbers on his chest to perform calculations.

PAGE 13

1a. 6 × 2 = total gallons of juice

1b. 12 gallons

2. 35 pies

3. 36 teaspoons

4. 33 bowls

5. 70 vitamins

6. 96 wings

7. 150 donuts

8a. Yes

8b. 13 pints less

PAGE 15

1. 9 pieces

2a. 12

2b. 15

2c. 6

3a. 15 feet

3b. 30 links

4. 480 cats

5a. 45 pounds

5b. 15 pounds

6. 30 days

PAGE 17

1a. 85 points

1b. 4 scores

1c. 21.3 points

2. 23.3 points

3. 18.8 points

4. 14.3 points

5. 16.0 points

6. 12.6 points

7. 10.9 points

8. 27 points

PAGE 19

1. Yes

2. No

3. Yes

4. No

5. Yes

6. 12

7. 6, 13, 33

8. 1, 2, 3, 4, 6, 8, 12, 16, 24, 48

9. 1, 2, 3, 4, 5, 6, 10, 12, 15, 20, 30, 60

10. 73 days

PAGE 21

1a. 1, 3, 5, 9, 15, 45

1b. 1, 3, 7, 9, 21, 63

1c. 9

2. 5

3. 8

4. 7

5. 22

6. 1

7. 39

8. 3

9. 14

10. 32

PAGE 23

1a. 4, 8, 12, 16, 20

1b. 6, 12, 18, 24, 30

1c. 12

2. 45

3. 27

4. 66

5. 260

6. 42

7. 120

8. 39

PAGES 25

1a. 4

1b. 3

1c. $4 \times 4 \times 4$

1d. 64

2. 32

3. 49

4. 729

5. 4,096

6. 97

7. 1

8. 1

9. 11^2

10. 3^4 or 9^2

PAGE 27

1a. 10

1b. $\frac{4}{10} \div \frac{5}{10}$

1c. $\frac{9}{10}$ of a pound

2. $\frac{9}{12}$ $\left(\frac{3}{4}\right)$ of a bowl

3. $\frac{1}{8}$ of a teaspoon

4. $\frac{19}{21}$ of an hour

5. $\frac{11}{18}$ of a glass

6. $\frac{17}{110}$ of a leg

7. $\frac{23}{30}$ of a pie

8. $\frac{31}{36}$ of a plate

PAGE 29

1a. $\frac{28}{1}$

1b. $\frac{28}{1} \times \frac{4}{7} = \frac{112}{7}$

1c. $\frac{112}{7} \div \frac{7}{7} = \frac{16}{1}$

1d. 16

2. 21

3. 15

4. 28

5. 24

6. 2

7. $\frac{7}{15}$ or $\frac{14}{30}$

PAGE 31

1a. $\frac{7}{3}$

1b. $2\frac{1}{3}$

2. $5\frac{1}{2}$

3. $4\frac{1}{4}$

4. 6

5. $3\frac{3}{5}$

6. $2\frac{1}{12}$

7. $\frac{3}{95}$

8. $\frac{11}{80}$

PAGE 33

1a. 26.191 seconds

1b. 26.18 seconds

1c. Millie Meedur's team

1d. .011 seconds

2a. .644 meters

2b. .641 meters

2c. Farrah's; .003 meters

3a. .195 pounds

3b. .196 pounds

3c. Carrie .001 pounds

4. Flip Ohverr won by .002 points.

5. B

PAGE 35

1a. 1.12 seconds

1b. 168.00 (168) pounds

2. 255.073 pounds

3. 59.984 pounds

4. 438.2284 pounds

5. 61.7652 pounds

6. 953.19 pounds

7. 750.9197 pounds

PAGE 37

1. $41.00

2. $26.75

3. $42.00

4. $75.72

5. $29.56; $17.70; Total cost: $47.26

6. $100.20; $34.23; $33.66; Total cost: $168.09

7. 3 maps, 4 books

PAGE 39

1a. .57

1b. 42.18

1c. 42 kangaroo-bots

2. 16 vampire bat-bots

3. 5 rhino-bots

4. 12 piranha-bots

5. 79 octo-bots

6. 39 panda-bots

7. 99 arachno-bots

8. About 32% (32.38242 . . .%)

PAGE 41

1. Pentagon

2. Heptagon

3. Triangle

4. Decagon

5. Nonagon

6. Hexagon

7. Octagon

8. Decagon

9. Pentagon

10. DODECAGON

PAGE 43

1. cat

2. runner

3. boat

4. candle

5. house

6. skater

7. rabbit

8. dancer

PAGE 45

1a. Perimeter = (3 feet + 7 feet) $\times$ 2

1b. 20 feet

1c. Area = 3 feet $\times$ 7 feet

1d. 21 square feet

1e. 14 feet

1f. 10 square feet

2a. 28 feet

2b. 48 square feet

3a. 40 inches

3b. 51 square inches

4a. 60 feet

4b. 224 square feet

5. 27 inches

6. 24 feet

7. 27 inches

PAGE 47

1a. $V = \frac{4}{3} \times \pi \times 3 \times 3 \times 3$

1b. 113.04 cubic feet

2. 523.33 cubic feet

3. 4,186.67 cubic feet

4. 1,436.03 cubic feet

5. 9,198.11 cubic feet

6. 24,416.64 cubic feet

7. 50,939.17 cubic feet

8. 28,716.35 cubic feet

PAGE 49

1a. 1,380 ÷ 60 = hours in 1,380 minutes

1b. 23 hours

2. 435 gallons

3. 189 pounds

4. 42 days

5. 91 years old

6. 17 miles

7. 94 megabytes

8. 22,000 pounds

PAGE 51

1a. $\frac{1}{8} = \frac{x}{56}$

1b. $x = 7$ inches

2. 1.95 inches

3. 1.1 inches

4. 2 inches

5. 2.6 inches

6. 7.2 inches

7. 35.2 inches

8. 122.5 feet

PAGE 53

1. Center City

2a. 1,000,000 ants

2b. 500,000 ants

3a. 11,000,000 ants

3b. 9,500,000 ants

4a. 3,000,000 more ants

4b. 5,500,000 more ants

5. Center City

6. 54,000,000 ants

7. 108 super heroes

8.

How Many of Each Food Item Needed

Bananas: (7 baskets)

PB&J Sandwiches: (5½ baskets)

Hot Dogs: (4 baskets)

Bags of Chips: (2½ baskets)

PAGE 55

BLUE SHIRT, RAINBOW SHORTS,
AND SUNGLASSES

(2, 5) (-2, 4) (2, 1) (-2, -3) (-6, -4) (-4, 3) (2, 5)

(-2, 4) (0, 3) (-2, 4) (1, 0) (-2, -3)

(-2, 4) (-6, 6) (-2, 4) (-4, 3) (0, 3)

PAGE 57

1. 13 feet

2a. Add 23

2b. Divide by 2

2c. 40 pounds

3. 30 gallons

4. 2 hours

5. 11 minutes

6. 63 miles

PAGE 59

1. 57 miles

2a. 60

2b. 12

3. 9 pounds, 6 ounces

4. 5 minutes